MORNING COFFEE THOUGHTS

A BOOK OF POEMS
ABOUT MY LOVE OF COFFEE
BY LOUISE NOTTINGHAM

ISBN-13: 978-1503257665

ISBN-10: 1503257665

Thank you, David,
for bringing me coffee,
almost every morning,
in bed.
You are the best!

The Sun is Shining

The sun is shining into my face
I sit up in bed and ask for grace
I beg forgiveness for my sins
And thus my day is about to begin

Rolling out of bed, I stand up,
Down stairs I go to fill my cup
Of coffee the thing that brings me joy
And starts my brain, sleep to destroy

Outside the sun brightly shines
And I wonder, what is the time
Do birds that sing have coffee too
Perhaps they do perhaps they do

Interesting thoughts pop in and pop out
Another cup of coffee should release all doubt
And then my day will really begin
I will dress, and smile, today I will win!

Coffee Haiku #1

Sleep time is over
I need a cup of coffee
Awake time is here

The Coffee Pot Is Cold

I stumble to the kitchen
And the coffee pot is cold
I start my day growling and bitchen
I stumble to the kitchen
In cabinets I look for the fixens
To make me feel more bold
I stumble to the kitchen
And the coffee pot is cold

Coffee Haiku #2

Where is the coffee?
Could it be that there is none?
Oh what will i do?

A Cup Of Coffee – One Poem, Two Voices

A cup of coffee would taste good right now
With hot with steam rising high above it
It is my morning mantra, of this I do avow

It is early in the morning when I enjoy my sacred Tao
I am really nothing without it, I heartedly admit
A cup of coffee would taste good right now

Sometimes I adorn it with cream from a cow
Sometimes I prefer the cream to omit
It is my morning mantra, of this I do avow

Inside my cat sits beside me, softly singing a meow
While life outside my door, can throw me a fit
A cup of coffee would taste good right now

Coffee helps me to soften life's and sin I disavow
In calming voice and between sips, I pray my commit
It is my morning mantra, of this I do avow

I think of all the things I must do and I wonder how
I will ever get them all done, who will get me through it
A cup of coffee would taste good right now
It is my morning mantra, of this I do avow

Coffee Haiku #3

Hot black sweet coffee
Caffeine is a gift from god
Raise a glass and sip

The Coffee Pot Sings Good Morning

pht pht shhhh spt
The coffee pot sings good morning
pht pht shhhh spt
A cup of coffee poured for me
Add some chocolate and honey
Sit and sip and enjoy it now
pht pht shhhh spt

pht pht shhhh spt
The coffee pot sings good morning
pht pht shhhh spt
I feel the coffee slide down my throat
I think I feel it it my veins
I am ready to start the day
pht pht shhhh spt

pht pht shhhh spt
The coffee pot sings good morning
pht pht shhhh spt
Another cup of coffee please
Add more chocolate and honey
Out the door, I take it and run
pht pht shhhh spt

Coffee Haiku #4

Decaffeinated
Is an ugly tired sad word
Give me some caffeine!

I Need A Cup Of Coffee

I need a cup of coffee
But the cupboards are coffeeless and bare
I need a cup of coffee
To brighten my dull blank stare

If I go for a pound of coffee
I should add sweetener to the list
And a little bit of chocolate
Would definitely add some bliss

If I have coffee with chocolate
Then why not a cookie or two
Oatmeal with chocolate chips and icing
That would be something to look forward to!

I need a cup of coffee
And cream is rich but not much of a treat
Now whipped cream sprayed into a high peak
Could be a seductively wonderful tweak

I need a cup of coffee
Which means I need to get dressed
Maybe just sweat pants, t-shirt and ball cap
After all there's no one there I want to impress

I need a cup of coffee!

Coffee Haiku #5

Before the birds sing
My dear love makes me coffee
I pretend to sleep

Coffee

Comfort in a cup
Oddly bland and yet very refreshing
Flavorful without having much flavor
Frill for the frilless
Enjoyable moments, sip by sip
Energy, strength and stamina building

Coffee Haiku #6

Sweet morning bird songs
Lull me to sleep all day long
Coffee to move me

Sitting Sipping Coffee

The yard was full of rose petals
The bushes were nearly bare
But then something happened
Pink flowers erupted everywhere

It's so nice to sit and look
Out my windows each day
In my quiet little house
I sit and watch the birds at play

Sipping coffee still warm
From earlier this morn
Pondering life's questions
As i look at rose bushes adorned

The yard was full of rose petals
The bushes were nearly bare
Sitting and sipping my coffee
Into the backyard i stare

Coffee Haiku #7

One get up and go on
Served in a clean china cup
Now this is coffee

Road Trip

Riding
Riding in a car
Riding in a car with classical music on
Yawning
Yawning again
Yawning again and again is contagious
Stopping
Stopping for coffee
Stopping for coffee and a large fry
Riding
Riding in a car
Riding in a car with coffee, large fries, and classical music on
Yawn

Coffee Haiku #8

How do people start
Each day without fresh coffee
Even stale would do

I Need Coffee

To
Start
The day
Without coffee
Is a terrible thing to do
It causes so much frustration
It causes headaches too
The world around is
Just a foggy blur
A day started
Without a
Cup of
Coffee
No
Thank
You sir!
Let all those
Who decaffeinate
Avoid me while I have a
Cup to change my dreary state
Leave me alone to whine and moan
Ignore my unpleasant before coffee groan
Or just to go back to sleep
I beg of you bleep bleep bleep
I need my coffee!

Coffee Haiku #9

Strong cappuccino
Slowly steeped in a French press
Topped with some frothed milk

Wobbly Stood

Standing up just out of bed
Wobbly there I stood
Creeping to the kitchen door
For some coffee hot to pour

Sipping slowly first I did
Slowly opening just one eyelid
Peeking out to see the day
This one good I hope I pray

Coffee Haiku #10

Mocha java, yum
A smooth dark cup with some rum
This could lead to fun

A Busy Day Starts With

A busy day starts with
One cup of coffee
And a broken coffee carafe
A clock too fast
A missing shoe
A gazillion questions
From a gazillion people
Hugs and kisses from daughter
And please mama please
And homework that's not quite right
A husband on the road
A stomach that's growling
And the knowledge
That tomorrow
If I am lucky
I get to do it all over
Again!

Coffee Haiku #11

A teaspoon of sweet
In my coffee is a treat
Sweets for the sweetest!

I Have A Lot To Do

I have a lot to do today
A lot of work, very little play
A lot of coffee to keep sleep at bay
I have a lot to do today
A quick stop at a breakfast buffet
Then the laundry, the library and a child's play
I have a lot to do today
A lot of work, very little play

Coffee Haiku #12

My cup is empty
And the coffee pot is too
I will make some more.

Coffee

Coffee in the morning is really good
Coffee with lunch is understood
Coffee cold with cream and something sweet
Is a wonderful afternoon treat!

Coffee before dinner is a must
Coffee after dinner decaffeinated I trust
Coffee flavored ice cream will make me scream
So much coffee that it's in my dreams!

Coffee Haiku #13

Coffee is downstairs
My empty cup is upstairs
I am so tired

I Can't Believe

I can't believe the coffee pot
Was dry as the desert
I can't believe I stayed awake
Long enough for dessert

I can't believe I made it home
Safely and in one piece
I can't believe that the day is done
And it's now time for sleep

Coffee Haiku #14

Coffee flavored sweets
Coffee ice cream and yogurt
Coffee all day long!

Coffee In The Morning

I love coffee in the morning
It brings
My mind
Into focus
The smell
Excites me
The taste
Soothes me
And that first sip is like ambrosia
I love coffee in the morning

I need coffee in the afternoon
It awakens
My sleep
Craved body,
The smell
Brings the
World into
Needed focus
And each sip gives me hope
I need coffee in the afternoon

I can't drink coffee after 5pm
Or I
Am up
Wide awake
All night
Long
I definitely without a doubt
Cannot drink coffee after 5pm

But
I love coffee in the morning!

Coffee Haiku #15

Coffee is a bean
And beans are vegetables
So coffee is soup.

First Task – Coffee

Early
While the sun still sleeps
My brain wakes
Before
My eyes
Before
My ears
Before
My arms and legs
My brain begins its day
A task list is made
So
That
When i arise
My feet will hit the ground
And my body
Still sore and tired from the day before
Knows
It's duties for the day
First task
Make
Coffee

Coffee Haiku #16

A cup of clever
To start my busy today
No nappies for me

Little Coffee Poem

Coffee in the morning
To start my boring day
Coffee in the afternoon
Awake it helps me stay
Coffee after 5pm
Is a stupid thing to drink
Coffee drunk later
And i won't sleep a wink!

Coffee Haiku #17

If no one makes a
Fresh pot of coffee at two
Nap at three past noon

I Slept In Late

This morning i slept in late
To over sleep is sometimes great
But today was in the way
Of to-do lists i had for the day
So in my haste to make up time
I sat and wrote this poem of mine
And sipped my coffee with pleasure
And daydreamed of writing treasures
And then at the clock i did look
It was time to read a book

Coffee Haiku #18

Post meridiem
And ante meridiem
Are great for coffee

Good Morning

Good morning morning of today
Coffee i need before we play
A cup as large as i can find
With enough caffeine to wake my mind

Today sipping just won't do
I need a straw to drink through
This fog in my brain is very thick
I hope caffeine sucked down will do the trick

Eventually i will awake
And then something creative I will make
Good morning morning, coffee cup in hand
I know that today will be grand!

Coffee Haiku #19

Afternoon doldrums
Depress the mind and body
Coffee is the cure

Coffee in Rhyming Triolet

Whether my coffee comes hot
Or in an icy frothy creamy tall venti bought
It makes difference to me, not
Whether my coffee comes hot
With one or two or even three extra shots
Coffee can reverse my discontent in a pot
Whether my coffee comes hot
Or in an icy frothy creamy tall venti bought

Coffee Haiku #20

Tall, grande, venti,
Is there really a best choice?
Yes, venti of course!

Coffee Is Amazing To Wake My Sleepy Head.

I never, well hardly ever, hear the alarm
And when I do, I do my best to it, unarm!
Happiness is having a coffee pot next to my bed,
Coffee is amazing to wake my sleepy head.

Sounds to not really wake me from a deep sleep
You can yell at me or blast a horn, I will remain in a heap
But the smell of coffee open my eyes of red
Coffee is amazing to wake my sleepy head.

Coffee's energy never does long last
But lucky for me, I agree to have more, when asked.
Caffeine is the drug of energy, the internet said
Coffee is amazing to wake my sleepy head.

Without a fresh cup of coffee in the morning I am a mess
And several cups at noon and one and I feel blessed.
I just want to say to those reading this thread,
Coffee is amazing to wake my sleepy head.

Coffee Haiku #21

In a china cup
Doesn't change the taste of it.
Coffee is coffee.

Decaffeinated

Why does anyone bother with decaffeinated coffee
When everyone knows it's the sugar that will kill you!
No caffeine simply creates a world of zombies
Why does anyone bother with decaffeinated coffee
Without it my personality is awfully wishy washy
And awfully nasty scary too!
Why does anyone bother with decaffeinated coffee
When everyone knows it's the sugar that will kill you!

Coffee Haiku #22

Do you feel run down
When the clock counts down to one?
I need coffee times two!

China Coffee Cup

A china cup with tiny pink flowers
And real gold painted on the rim
I could sit and sip for hours
From a china cup with tiny pink flowers
Happy inside while outside stormy showers
Frothed high with milk 2% skim
A china cup with tiny pink flowers
And real gold painted on the rim

Coffee Haiku #23

Sometimes I don't want
A big hot cup of coffee
Sometimes I want iced!

She Was Scary And Odd

I met a person who was cheerful
And didn't eat or drink caffeine.
I stood away from her, for I was fearful.
I met a person who was cheerful,
If I didn't have coffee, I would be tearful,
It is the fuel of this beautiful machine!
I met a person who was cheerful
And didn't eat or drink caffeine.
She scares me.

Coffee Haiku #24

Often I snooze the
Alert sound starting my day.
Strong coffee needed

A Coffee Rondelet

Some coffee please,
I start my day with some coffee
Some coffee please,
Make it tall, sweet, strong and frothy
Kamikaze, salty, toffee
I need it now, coffee jockey!
Some coffee please.

Coffee Haiku #25

Iced coffee with some
Whipped cream, chocolate, and caramel
A diet killer

Morning Waitress Do Not Pass My Table By

Morning waitress do not pass my table by
Carrying the pitcher of hot elixir of joy
Carrying the fuel for with I cry

Waitress I beg you to not rush by
Do not with my emotions toy
Morning waitress do not pass my table by

Anxiously I sit, fidgeting, quietly I sigh
Maybe you would stop if I were a cute boy
Carrying the fuel for with I cry

Wildly and silently I plot, my cup still dry
Your own joy I may soon destroy
Morning waitress do not pass my table by

I beg, I plead, I vow, you will comply
My cup will be full, caffeine you will deploy
Carrying the fuel for with I cry

I sit and sob for my soul, about to die
All I want is some coffee to enjoy
Morning waitress do not pass my table by
Carrying the fuel for with I cry

Coffee Haiku #26

I woke to the birds
Arguing about something.
I sip my Coffee

When Coffee Goes On Sale

When coffee goes on sale
And you live up north
Where weather often turns
To a blinding white gale
You quickly learn to stock up
On the ambrosia that fills the morning cup
When coffee goes on sale
And you live up north.

Coffee Haiku #27

Morning first aid kit
Coffee, chocolate pastry
Poetry and time.

Coffee Queen

I
Have
A favorite
Glass coffee cup
That i think morning
Coffee tastes best in when
Served to me while still in bed
Sadly, i do not think that my
Husband agrees with nor
Does he seem to care
At least not enough
To bring me some
Coffee in that
Special cup
To wake
Me
But he does still bring to me
While still in bed a wonderful
Hot cup of coffee
I am his queen!

Coffee Haiku #28

Two o'clock every
Afternoon I want a nap
Coffee fixes that

What Do You Like In Your Coffee?

What do you like in your coffee?
Teaspoons or tablespoons of sweet?
What do you like in your coffee?
Do you like your coffee black or white?
Do you take it with two percent milk?
Or do you prefer full thick, heavy, cream?
What do you like in your coffee?
Will you order coffee plain or with flavor?
Do you dance with joy when pumpkin spice
Finally becomes seasonally available?
Does white chocolate peppermint mocha
Make your heart pound with joy,
Mouth salivate in anticipation?
What do you like in your coffee?

Coffee Haiku #29

My cat does not drink
Coffee but does like the smell.
He inhales, I drink.

Dread

Fan spinning over my head
Another day to start - get out of bed
Starting without coffee is what i dread
Fan spinning over my head
Happy thoughts and plans instead
Fan spinning over my head
Another day to start - get out of bed

Coffee Haiku #30

When I cannot have
Coffee to drink, I do not cry
Try coffee ice cream!

Late Night Coffee

Decaffeinated coffee is just a trick
It does nothing
In the morning, it makes me sick
But late at night
When I am tired but tense
I might drink a cup
For comfort and joy and quiet my sense

Decaffeinated coffee is not real
It is a mask,
a useless copy of morning elixir without appeal
But late at night
When a person wants to try to sleep
I might drink a cup
So my date with dreams I might keep

Good night.